David Lassman has generated free publicity through the med print around the world. He has into this seven step guide *The* reveals the secrets behind his mo

'PR stunts don't get much better than this' – *Lewis PR global consultancy*

'The literary story of 2007' – *Western Daily Press*

'A cheeky experiment' – *The Guardian*

'A self-publicist who has turned his skill into an art form' – *Bath Chronicle*

For Claire
*Thanks for all your support and
for keeping my ego healthy*

The Art of Self-Publicity

by

David Lassman

Writers' Workshop
Guide No.1

Published by Writers' Workshop, an imprint of Awen Publications, 7 Dunsford Place, Bath, England BA2 6HF

www.awenpublications.co.uk

Copyright ©David Lassman 2010

David Lassman has asserted his right to be identified as the author of this Work in accordance with the Copyright, Designs and Patents Act 1988

All rights reserved. No part of this publication may be reproduced, stored in a retrieval system, or transmitted in any form or by any means, electronic, mechanical, photocopying, recording or otherwise, without the prior permission of the copyright owner.

A CIP catalogue record for this book is available from the British Library

ISBN: 978-1-906900-14-4

Author website: www.davidlassman.com

ACKNOWLEDGEMENTS

I want to thank the following people for their involvement, either directly or indirectly, in the writing process and production of the book you hold in your hand. **Kevan** for publishing this book, for all that preceded it and for a continuing and inspiring friendship; **Claire** for her unfailing support of, and belief in, my creative journey – of which this book is one expression and its dedication a small, if thoroughly deserved, gesture; **Joanna** for writing the foreword; everyone who have participated in the workshops and talks over the years – your feedback has been invaluable; and finally to all the radio stations, television channels, newspapers, magazines and other media outlets around the world that have been so accommodating in giving over their column inches and their airtime.

FOREWORD
by Joanna Crosse

I was delighted to be asked to write this foreword as I have worked with David on a number of occasions and have always found his approach to be direct yet perceptive.

My own work as a voice and presentation coach includes the area of self-publicity and I am only too aware how most of us find it difficult to sell ourselves.

This book is a useful, as well as entertaining, guide for anyone who wants to raise their profile or achieve publicity for their work. It distils the years of experience David has accumulated gaining media coverage and exposure and is packed full of real life anecdotes, practical exercises and advice.

If anyone should have written this book it is David. Although having successfully worked with organisations and businesses large and small, his own track record of self-publicity ranges from local radio stations to American television networks and from regional magazines to international newspapers.

David has been there and done it, and whether you are just starting out or already established, I am certain you will benefit from this practical guide to the art of self-publicity.

***

Joanna Crosse has achieved a high profile as a voice and presentation coach and has worked for many of the national media organisations, including ITV, BBC and Channel 4. She is also the author of the best-selling book *Find Your Voice – how clear communication can transform your life.*

CONTENTS

Introduction..7

Step One: Befriend your Ego................................10

Step Two: What's your Product?........................17

Step Three: Know your Reason............................25

Step Four: Find the Angle.....................................31

Step Five: Create the Buzz....................................39

Step Six: Become Number One............................46

Step Seven: Sustaining your Profile....................56

. . . And Finally...62

INTRODUCTION

The idea for this book has arisen quite naturally I believe, from workshops I have run on the subject and through feedback I have received from those participating in them. The workshops themselves are largely based on my own experiences, along with observations of several other self-publicists who seem to effortlessly gain media coverage for some event or other.

This guide can therefore be seen as an extension of the workshop material, albeit expanded, and yet existing as its own separate entity. The practical exercises I have devised for the workshops are also included and I am confident everything required to set you off on the path of obtaining self-publicity is contained within these covers.

So what exactly is the Art of Self-Publicity? Is it making something out of nothing, a way of never paying for advertising again, or the result of an active ego? Well, it is all these things and more but first we need to define exactly what these terms mean within the context of this book.

The word *Art* relates to a skill, aptitude, or knack of being able to do something well. This ability is usually attained and honed through practise and knowledge of the particular subject. *Self* is by, or for, oneself, relating to each of us as individuals; and *Publicity* is the exposure of a product, company or person, with the aim of deriving benefit from this exposure.

Therefore the Art of Self-Publicity is about developing one's own ability to create the necessary exposure for whatever it is you wish to gain benefit from. As most of the people who attend my workshops are creative or artistic types – musicians, writers, painters – I will use the term 'artist' to encompass the complete range of creative endeavours, although this book will, I hope, be useful for anyone who has a message to tell the world.

The book is structured so as to lead you initially to an awareness of the resources you already have available to you and identifying what it is you have to promote, on through the production of material designed to gain the media interest and secure coverage, and finally onto what to do once you have achieved a level of success and how to sustain it.

There are seven steps to learning the Art of Self-Publicity and as you progress your way through them there are the aforementioned practical exercises. These are designed to help identify your individual requirements and, as most, if not all, of the time there is very little or no budget for promotion or PR, allow you to develop your initiative.

But apart from only ever personally paying ninety pence for advertising, and running the workshops, you may be wondering what gives me the credentials to be writing a book such as this.

My own forays into self-publicity began in the mid-1980s when I started an appreciation society for a long dead rock star (more of that later). In the quarter of a century that has elapsed since then, I have carved out a career in gaining publicity for both myself and others. During that time many of the modes of communication have changed quite dramatically but whatever modern technology and new opportunities to gain media coverage have arisen, the basics of self-publicity never change and it is these that form the seven steps that make up this guide.

Throughout my career I have written, edited and produced articles, newsletters, magazines, press releases and other promotional material for a diverse range of organisations including education establishments, commercial enterprises, newspapers & periodicals, and an array of leisure orientated and tourism-related businesses. During this time I have held various positions such as communications officer, press & PR manager, festival director, entertainments editor and arts columnist.

This is in addition to my own projects, including the self-publicity workshops, through which I have spoken at events and festivals and given interviews for radio and television stations around the world, as well as having my name in print in every English national daily newspaper.

Probably my biggest achievement in terms of self-publicity, however, was in 2007 when I created the literary story of the year - according to at least one newspaper - and my name and image was briefly known worldwide, gaining an estimated £1 million pounds worth of free publicity for myself and the organisation I was working for at the time (but again, more of that later).

But this book is about you and how you can learn the rules of self-publicity in order to go out in the marketplace, make a noise, raise your profile and gain some publicity for yourself.

So, ready? Right, let's do it ...

David Lassman,
Bath, March 2010

STEP ONE

BEFRIEND YOUR EGO

As we learnt in the introduction the Art of Self-Publicity, at least as defined in the context of this book, is about developing your own ability to create the necessary exposure for whatever it is you wish to gain benefit from.

The ways to achieve the 'art' and 'publicity' of the title will be discussed in forthcoming chapters, but step one is about the second part of the phrase, that of the self, and looking at its position within the process of gaining publicity and promoting oneself.

It may seem obvious but the point does need to be made that at this stage it is you who holds the key to starting out on this process of getting yourself and your work known and out there, and not the media, publishing companies, gallery owners or such like.

Why is this so? Well, I believe it is because as artists there is often a resistance to the raising one's profile and a natural reticence not to publicise any work. This is perhaps due to two reasons.

Firstly, the act of creating is an interior process, often solitary, inward looking and introspective and so while in other aspects of life we may be more outward going and naturally sociable, where our creative work is concerned the act of creation is an act of exposing our nature and so we find any aspect of discussing this work painful or embarrassing.

And secondly, this reluctance is due to the belief that if we are seen to be actively promoting ourselves it is in somehow egotistical; that commercial ambition goes against the creative spirit and compromises artistic integrity, and that any work should succeed on its own merits.

The two points are interrelated but in regard to the second point, that of negating commercial ambition, consider this: as artists we are perhaps one of the most egotistically-minded and commercially ambitious people there is. Why? Well, I feel this is due to the fact that even though it may be through a genuine creative impulse we produce all of our poetry, paintings, novels or songs, the moment we begin to submit them to publishers, agents or record companies the ego is at work and commercial ambition has surfaced.

We send our work out in the belief that whoever receives it is going to be impressed enough to say 'yes' to us, whether that is agreeing to publish us, act as our agent, offering a recording deal or whatever. And that these people will then set about getting it ready to put out to an eager public only too willing to spend their hard earned cash on our product and their precious time reading, listening or gazing upon what we have created. And afterwards, telling all their friends about how good it is.

There is nothing wrong with this and if we did not have that belief in our work we shouldn't be sending it out in the first place, but the point I am making is that we have to become aware that there is an ego at work - we would not be able to create anything without one - it is just that most of the time we want someone else to take responsibility for it.

Therefore, the first step we have to take is to resolve the issue surrounding our ego, in order to focus on the job at hand – that of promoting ourselves and our work. Of course, a boastful, egocentric person is usually a bore and people who become overly confident can often become arrogant.

But this is the shadow of the ego, or what is known as an unhealthy ego, whereas someone who uses the ego in the right way - a healthy ego - is being self-confident and can achieve nearly anything they put their mind to.

So what I am talking about is using the ego as a driving force to achieve your objective – whatever that is. Used correctly, it is the most powerful tool you have available for fulfilling your dreams and realising your aspirations. I believe a healthy ego is one that is exercised regularly but like actual physical exercise, this has to be done in a disciplined and ordered way.

And as your ego is the best ally you have, so you must make friends with it. As best-selling author Jodi Picoult has said "you've got to be your own cheerleader". You have to be. No one else will work as hard for you. Through using the ego effectively you can also create greater self-esteem, self-worth and self-belief. In the end, if you don't believe in yourself or your work, why should anyone else. You therefore have to overcome any shyness and recognise your own value.

In terms of psychology it was Freud who first labelled the ego, although it is the work of another psychologist, Carl Jung, whose insights are most important to this section. Jung wrote that "the ego is the fragile, precious light of consciousness that must be guarded and cultivated [as it] is our sense of purpose and identity." He believed the ego is related to what he called the persona - derived from the Latin for 'theatre mask' - and this persona is what we wear when interacting within society and is closely linked with self-esteem.

Self-esteem is another psychological term and is used to reflect a person's overall evaluation or appraisal of their own worth. It encompasses beliefs (e.g. "I am competent or incompetent") and emotions (triumph or despair, pride or shame), while certain behaviour may also stem from it such as assertiveness or shyness and confidence or caution.

The popular psychiatrist and media personality Professor Raj Persaud has theorized that true self confidence comes from an attitude where you "promise yourself, no matter how difficult the problem life throws at you, that you will try as hard as you can to help yourself. You acknowledge that sometimes your efforts to help yourself may not result in success, as often being properly rewarded is not in your control."

Whilst teaching how to boost self-esteem and self-confidence is outside the remit of this book, there are many books out there which will show you have to increase it and maintain it. I suggest that you do, because if you want to become successful in the Art of Self-Publicity, you have to believe in yourself and your work and put value on it. So, as it has been succinctly put "when we value ourselves and see our work as worthwhile, we make it much easier for others to form the same opinion."

What it comes down to in the end is to have enough self-belief to be able to promote yourself and your work to the outside world. Without that, it will very difficult to achieve any level of success. Or as John Bird, founder of the Big Issue, sees it "The more you believe in your idea, the better you will be able to sell it."

There are exceptions but these are rare. Mike Oldfield is one example. Choosing to become a recluse after recording *Tubular Bells,* he famously refused to do any promotion or publicity for it and subsequent releases. And yet every album he recorded during the following fifteen years reached the top ten.

Having said this, however, it must be mentioned that Oldfield was signed to Virgin records, whose boss at the time was Richard Branson, acknowledged to be one of the great self-publicists. His PR stunts have been numerous over the years, as he knows that they will make the difference between a story about one of his companies ending up in the business pages or the front pages.

So the truth of the matter is that unless you can find someone like Richard Branson to work for you, you're more than likely have to go out there ourselves to achieve publicity. But first, we need to identify what exactly it is we are going to take out there to the world.

Always remember . . .

1. Commercial ambition and artistic integrity are not necessarily incompatible.

2. A healthy ego is the greatest driving force to help reach an ambition.

3. The ego is your personal cheerleader and number one fan.

4. If you value your work, it is easier for others to do so likewise.

5. Publicity-shy artists that achieve success are rare.

AS SEEN AT:

'The Art of Self-Publicity' WORKSHOP

Learn how to promote yourself, your business or your creative output.

A three-hour workshop with David Lassman that includes practical exercises and bespoke advice. Book now on 07804 246931 or email at david@davidlassman.com

SATURDAY 17TH OCTOBER 2009

Bath Central Library, 19-23 The Podium, Bath, BA1 5AN

A few of the media outlets David Lassman has achieved coverage include:
Good Morning America, BBC's One Show, BBC World Service, News at Ten CNN, Channel 4, New York Times, The Guardian, The Times, Radio 4 The Independent, The Observer, Radio 5 Live and The Today Show

'A self-publicist who has turned his skill into an art form'
- BATH CHRONICLE

STEP TWO

WHAT'S THE PRODUCT ?

Once you have self-belief in place, you can move to the next stage and begin preparations for entering the market place. As we saw in the previous chapter, there can be a reluctance to think about yourself or your work as a product, something to be clinically bought and sold, but this is exactly what is needed.

If there is reluctance a new paradigm of thinking is required, because whichever industry is relevant to you – publishing, music, fashion – that is exactly what it is. And the nature of any industry is fundamentally commercial. Businesses, corporations or giant conglomerates, be they record companies, book publishers, art galleries or whatever, exist to make money, they have to, or else they will not survive.

If this whole business of commerciality really does seem to be so abhorrent then you have to stop and ask one question: if that is the case then why are *you* trying to become part of that particular industry.

In certain ways this is perhaps the most difficult stage to take on board, yet one when accepted will yield the greatest possibilities. It may be hard but if you can understand this need to think in terms of products then, along with your self-belief, you are on your way, or at least have taken the first major step, to achieving your aim - that of gaining publicity for whatever it is you want to bring to the world's attention.

However, let me make it clear that I am not advocating painting, writing, composing or whatever you do, solely for money. If this is the only reason you are doing whatever it is you do, then you would be well advised to seek another avenue with a more guaranteed and regular income! This is about vocation, because if you don't have it you will be knocked back, put off, or disillusioned very quickly.

But if vocation alone was enough, then you would not need this book. You would be happy and content to carry on in your artistic endeavours with no burning desire to communicate your creative output to a wider audience. And if this did happen, it would be more serendipity than by design.

Here lies the rub then and the reason you have probably bought this book – whatever most artists think, somewhere they do want to bring their creations to a wider audience and to make money from doing so. And as I have said earlier about the ego, there is nothing wrong with this attitude.

Hopefully by now I have convinced you that you are entering a marketplace, so the next part of this stage is to identify exactly what you have to sell – what's the product – and who might be interested in buying it. As you may have guessed, we are now entering the world of marketing.

In marketing terms, a product is anything that can be offered to a particular market that satisfies a want or need. Products can be either tangible – a physical item - such as a novel, compact disc, sculpture, or intangible - a non-physical one - such as a performance, workshop or a service.

It can be a painful, although necessary, process to accept this commercial reality but once you have accepted it, and can identify what it is you are selling and the audience you are trying to sell it to, you can begin to focus more clearly on creating the tailored publicity to gain their interest.

So where do you begin? First we need to see how we identify our chosen field and find our own place in it. I will use the publishing industry as an example, but it can be applied to any industry.

The publishing industry divides the books it produces and the authors it publishes into fiction or non-fiction. From here, they are sub-categorised into genres such as historical, romantic, chick-lit and science-fiction. Publishing companies are acutely aware of these divisions. For example, they would not buy the rights to a science fiction novel and try to sell it to readers of historical romance. No, they specifically aim each book at the people they know from their research to be the book's target audience.

A target audience refers to the primary group of people that something, usually an advertising campaign, is aimed at appealing to. A target audience can be members of a certain age group, gender, marital status or socio-economic grouping, but certain combinations, for example men from twenty to thirty years old, are often a commonly used standard. Other groups, however, although not the main focus, may also be included.

You may well be wondering at this stage what marketing, target audiences, or demographics has got to do with self-publicity and gaining media exposure. Well, the answer is that it has a lot to do with it. Whether you like it or not, we as a society, just like the books, have been divided and sub-divided into various different groups and categories so that companies and businesses can sell us their products more effectively and efficiently through marketing.

Marketing is the process by which companies determine what products or services may be of interest to particular customers, and the strategy to use in sales, communications and business development. In short, marketing is used to identify the customer, to keep the customer and to satisfy the customer. These customers have usually been identified through research and, as mentioned previously, are known as a target audience.

Once you have identified your own target audience for your work, and it advisable to do so as soon as possible, it is essential to become familiar with their habits, behaviours, likes and dislikes. Identify their values, attitudes, beliefs and opinions. A lot of this information will have to be generalisation at this stage, but figuring out what newspapers or magazines your audience reads, can go a long way to establishing their profile.

You should go onto the internet and look up the various marketing research on newspapers and their readers, or similar angled and relevant industry reports by companies or trade magazines.

But first a practical exercise to learn more about yourself.

PROFILE QUESTIONNAIRE

Q1. Male / Female
Q2. Age group – under 18 / 18-25 / 26 - 35 / 36-55 / over 55
Q3. If you were a daily newspaper, what would it be?
Q4. In ten words or less describe what it is you do 'creatively'
Q5. What country would best reflect your personality?
Q6. Which actively best reflects your interest? Reading / Walking / Sunbathing / Cooking
Q7. What creative term is relevant to your work? Writer / Musician / Painter / Poet / Other (please list)
Q8. What would be your ideal evening? Night spent out with friends / romantic meal for two / trip to the cinema to see the latest film / night in with takeaway and telly / other (please list)
Q9. Within your creative field, what genre(s) best defines your art.
Q10. Describe your finished product? (e.g. novel, record)

This is an exercise to begin showing you how your profile can be compiled and the benefits from this. The more information you know about yourself, the greater effectiveness your efforts in gaining publicity will probably have.

Look at your answers and spend a little time thinking (and possiby writing) what they say about you. For example, question six, dependent on your answer (although there are no 'wrong' ones), reveals you to be an interior passive, exterior active, exterior passive or else interior active person.

(You can also use this questionnaire to compile a basic profile of your possible target audience.)

There are a number of useful demographic classifications that can help this process of identifying target audiences, although perhaps the most well-known are the NRS social grades, originally developed by the National Readership Survey in order to classify readers, but now standard for market research.

The grades are often grouped into ABC1 and C2DE and these are taken to equate to middle class and working class respectively. Only a very small percentage of the population is identified as upper class, and so this group is not included in the classification scheme.

This can be a useful tool for discovering the appropriate target audience(s) to which your product or service should be aimed but whatever you employ, it is imperative that you realise this is one of the most important stages involved in the process of gaining media exposure and coverage. Without knowing your target audience and who you are trying to appeal to, a lot of effort in trying to gain self-publicity may be wasted.

Once you have an idea of this target audience then you can also set about deciding how you wish to present yourself to this audience and how you would like to be perceived. As you will be perceived one way or the other by the audience, as well as by the world at large, you might has well have a hand in shaping this perception!

As William Wordsworth astutely appreciated some two hundred years ago "Every great and original writer, in proportion as he is great and original, must himself create the taste by which he is to be relished."

So, having begun to identify the target audience you are aiming at, and deciding the best types of media to use, you can begin to plan the specifics of your publicity campaign.

Always remember . . .

1. Whatever industry is relevant to you, it will be commercial to survive.

2. You will be in a stronger position to achieve your ambitions if you think in terms of product.

3. Artistic endeavours should strike a balance between the commercial and the vocational.

4. You are entering a marketplace and exactly what you are intending to offer the market needs to be identified clearly.

5. If you know your target audience you will find it easier to reach them.

STEP THREE
KNOW YOUR REASON

Self-publicity should always be gained for a reason, which means you need to identify what it is you want to publicise and what you want to achieve from this exposure. Leave self-publicity for self-publicity's sake to those merely craving media attention as an end in itself. Two contrasting examples of people who have achieved a high level of media coverage illustrate this point.

Karl Power achieved notoriety during the Noughties for publicity stunts that revolved around his appearing, uninvited, at sporting events. Probably the most famous of these occurring before a European football match in 2001, when he strode on to the pitch dressed in a Manchester United strip and took his place alongside the unsuspecting players for their team photograph.

Other appearances were staged at an England cricket game, a national rugby match, Wimbledon and during a British Grand Prix at Silverstone when he beat Michael Schumacher to the winners' podium. But aside from showing up security lapses at these major sporting events and having a documentary made about him, Power was seemingly more interested in gaining media coverage for the actual attention, rather than for promoting any product or building a career. In that sense, Power is more prankster than self-publicist.

Not so, Matt O'Connor. He founded the fathers' rights organisation Fathers 4 Justice (F4J) following separation from his wife and finding himself with only very limited access to his young sons. O'Conner (interestingly enough a marketing consultant) began a series of publicity stunts aimed at championing and bringing to the attention of the public, through the media, the cause of family law reform and equal contact for divorced parents with children.

These stunts usually involved scaling public buildings or monuments dressed as Father Christmas or comic superheroes. The use of high-profile and disruptive stunts garnered so much media coverage in the early days of the F4J, *The Times* wrote of the group that it "has succeeded in becoming the most prominent guerrilla pressure group in Britain . . . within eighteen months of its founding."

O'Connor's success also has been shown through the number of similar organisation that have since sprung up all around the world and although some of these have come in for criticism and negative publicity during their existence, what they all do best is staging dramatic protest stunts.

Probably the most notable publicity stunt I have so far created occurred in 2007, which involved Jane Austen and was referred to by *The Guardian* as a 'cheeky experiment'. This was my investigation to see whether the novelist, despite the millions of books sold and the countless film and television adaptations of them, would be able to find a publisher in today's world.

I sent out the opening chapters to three of her novels, including *Pride & Prejudice*, with only minor changes, to some of the UK's biggest publishers and agents. I used a pseudonym and gave the return address as 40 Gay Street, Bath (which is in fact the Jane Austen Centre). As *The Guardian* put it, I was "amazed when they all sent the manuscripts back with polite but firm 'no-thank-you's' and almost all failed to spot that he was ripping off one of the world's most famous literary figures."

The result was worldwide coverage and for a couple of days I found myself at the centre of a media 'storm'. I was thus able to promote the trio of reasons for which I had sought the publicity.

Firstly, to gain publicity for *Freedom's Temple*, my unpublished novel that had been universally rejected by most of the same publishers and agents a few months beforehand. Secondly to publicise the Jane Austen Festival, at the time being its director, and thirdly, to raise the profile of the Regency World magazine in which my 'Rejecting Jane' article had originally appeared.

One thing to remember before embarking on any publicity campaign, however, is to make sure whatever it is you want to publicise can be easily be accessed by the media and public. Therefore preparation is the key.

Is your manuscript in a word document? Are your songs available on the web? Could you send anything off straight away to a journalist, a publisher or record company after a phone call or an email? If a newspaper wants your press release, or a magazine wants a review copy can you send it to them immediately.

> **EXERCISE**
>
> **Q1. What exactly do you want to publicise?**
>
> **Q2. What would be the ideal outcome?**
>
> **Q3. What do you need to make sure is easily accessible before you start your publicity campaign?**
>
> **Q4. How will you make this available?**

The main element to the recent Susan Boyle 'phenomenon' – a supposed no-hoper who appeared on Britain's Got Talent and taught the judges and studio audience a lesson about pre-judgement - was that people could view the clip, often repeatedly, on You Tube; it was easily accessible to the world. Within a week of her performance and the resultant media coverage, the footage had generated tens of millions of hits (the ever increasing number of hits even became a news story in its own right after it overtook American President Barack Obama's inauguration speech).

Although Susan Boyle could not have been prepared for this huge publicity – indeed, she reputedly had not heard of You Tube - the makers of the television programme certainly were, or at least they were prepared enough to exploit the exposure when it happened. This exposure and subsequent exploitation has lead to front pages all over the world, interviews on high-profile chat shows, the biggest selling album of 2009 (even though it was only released six weeks before the end of the year) and the Britain's Got Talent brand raising its profile to the highest level.

The key point to remember is that when something does achieve media coverage, you have a small window of opportunity to make the most of it and to build something bigger from it.

Before that, however, you need to take the next step in the process of generating this publicity . . .

Always remember . . .

1. Self-publicity should always been undertaken for the promotion of you or your work.

2. Publicity stunts work best when combining the serious with the playful.

3. Always make sure whatever it is you are publicising is easily accessible.

4. Preparation is the key.

5. There is normally only a small window of opportunity arising from media coverage, so you have to be as ready as possible to capitalise on it.

STEP FOUR
FIND THE ANGLE

Now you know the product you want to publicise and are prepared for any possible media coverage, you have to find the part of your product which will get the media interested and allow them to produce a news story around it.

When presented with a possible story, media people, especially those in the news departments, always ask the same question "what's the angle?" What they mean by this is what element of your story or product makes it newsworthy, what will hook an audience into wanting to know more, what takes it out of the commonplace.

This is the 'man bites dog' scenario. If a dog bites a man, this being an everyday occurrence, it is not newsworthy, but if a man bites a dog, that's unusual and will no doubt create curiosity, leading to the question 'why did the man bite the dog?' and a desire to find out the answer.

Therefore you have to look at the product you want to gain publicity for and see if there is anything unusual about it which raises it above the commonplace. Is it the biggest, smallest, youngest, oldest, shortest, longest – in other words, what makes it stand out from the crowd and will make people curious to know more about it.

There is a practical exercise later in this section that will help identify possible angles. If after completing the questions you cannot find one, however, it is a case of creating something related to your product that does have an angle.

An example might be the launch of a book about basket weaving. This is probably not the most interesting piece of information any news desk will receive that day and therefore not of much note. However, if the book launch is organised around the biggest basket weaving event in the world, then you have created a potentially more newsworthy story.

When I took over the directorship of the Jane Austen Festival in 2007, which takes place in Bath each September, one of the first things I did was to look at the events already pencilled in, in order to judge those which had the most potential news 'value', as the angle or hook is often measured.

I decided it was the Grand Regency Promenade. This is where people from all around the world dress up in Regency costumes and parade through the streets of the city. It opens the festival and is very visual - so adding good photo opportunities to any story. However, as it was one of the regular events at the festival and had received coverage in previous years, it was therefore not 'new' and might possibly not warrant much interest on its own.

So to give it more news value I contacted the Guinness Book of World Records to ask if there was an existing record for the 'largest Regency promenade' we could attempt to break or, if not, they would accept ours if we created one. The application process is time-consuming but I felt it was worth it, as news stories based around world records are a staple of newsrooms (keep your eyes open to see how many stories you come across in the media that mention some kind of record).

Despite my efforts a world record attempt did not gain acceptance that year, mainly I believe, due to the fact the event did not have a charity attached to it and, as I had initially envisaged, therefore received, apart from a passing mention in the local paper, no media coverage.

My successor persevered though and on Saturday, September 19th, 2009, gathered 409 costumed people inside the Assembly Rooms, in Bath, during the promenade, and set the new world record for the 'largest gathering of people dressed in Regency costumes'. This time it did have a charity attached, the record was officially recognised, and a large media contingent was in attendance to ensure the event received coverage on radio, television and in print. This final point being extra satisfying on a personal level, as by that time I was the press & PR manager for the Jane Austen Centre, which organises the festival.

Another way to generate news value is by attaching your product or associated event with the famous or historical. Is there an anniversary associated with your product or can it be linked in some way to a person or monument already well-known.

Going back to the basket weaving book launch example - perhaps it is three hundred years since the birth of the person who invented basket weaving, or a top film actress has it as a secret hobby.

Back in the 1980s I started a music magazine called *Bath Beat*. It was named after *Mersey Beat*, the Liverpool music paper in the 1960s that first championed The Beatles (Editor Bill Harry was a friend of John Lennon). Someone had suggested a more regionalised name such as Out West, because as they rightly pointed out, the population of Liverpool to Bath is around a ratio of 5:1, but I stuck to my guns. I wanted to create that identification (however tenuous) and although the magazine only lasted a few issues (so in hindsight 'they' were probably right) it had achieved one of its main objectives, that of getting my profile raised enough to start writing music columns for the local newspaper.

Another music industry example is the U2 album *No Line on the Horizon*, released in 2009. It was their latest release and as such would expect to receive a large amount of publicity in the music press reserved for such a well-known band. Having decided to mount a bigger than usual PR campaign for this particular album, however, the band played a gig, or at least a couple of songs, on the roof of BBC Broadcasting House. Deliberately echoing The Beatles' rooftop performance atop Abbey Road Studios in 1969 (incidentally exactly thirty years before) which had become an iconic event in the annals of popular cultural. The mainstream media became interested and it gave the release widespread coverage.

One thing to remember is that the media is always looking to tie-in news stories with something or someone already well-known to its audience. For example, how many times have you read a news story likened to a successful film, popular television programme or a famous star?

But also remember, that the media are not beyond deliberately making up or distorting the facts to get a particular association.

On Wednesday April 22, 2009, for instance, one national newspaper ran a front page headline proclaiming '**Talent Susan: The Movie**'; alluding to Boyle-mania having now caught the interest of Hollywood. Underneath the main headline it then read in big bold letters: '**And Angelina Jolie is up for the lead role!**' For the full story you had to turn to pages 10 & 11 and once there, you found this most famous of actresses on a list – 'some of them cheeky' as the article admitted – of several film and television stars that *the paper itself* thought would be perfect for the role. The article's level of credibility reflected in that Robbie Coltrane was also a suggestion!

Another piece of media fabrication to gain an association came with the 'Battle of Britpop'. This was when Blur and Oasis – the two biggest music groups in the UK at the time – engaged in a battle for chart supremacy by releasing singles on the same day in 1995.

The music paper *New Musical Express*, or *NME*, referred to this race to see which band would secure the coveted number one slot in the following week's chart as the 'British Heavyweight Championship' and the showdown caught the media's attention. It gained national coverage, with the BBC's John Humphrys going so far as to excitedly announce on the Six o'clock news that 'the music industry hasn't seen anything like it since The Beatles fought it out with The Rolling Stones in the 60s.'

This of course was rubbish.

The Beatles and The Rolling Stones were more 'double act' than rivals, with respective group members ringing each other up when a new single was ready so as to plan staggered release dates. As the latter's guitarist Keith Richards put it, "there was a meticulous piece of work going on between The Beatles and The Stones to make sure we did not clash with each other."

EXERCISE

1. List anything that raises your product out of the commonplace

2. List one event you could create around your product

3. Find an association to the famous or historical

4. Find at least one world record associated with your artistic field (internet research or trip to the library might be called for this one)

At this point Andrew Loog Oldham, The Rolling Stones manager at the time, deserves a mention.

Having originally worked as a press agent for American rock & roll groups and then briefly for The Beatles themselves, Oldham took over management of The Rolling Stones in 1963. Savvy of the media and how to manipulate it, he actively promoted the 'bad boy' image the band became known for, through cultivating any bad moments the group inadvertently created or dreaming up headlines such as "Would you let your daughter marry a Rolling Stone?" As lead singer Mick Jagger admitted years later, "we used to visit hospital and visit sick children but it was never highlighted."

And it is not just fabrication or distortion the media engage in. Changing the angle to make better copy or even create another story is illustrated by the final example in this section.

The headline one national daily newspaper used for an article about the Manuel-gate saga read *'Andrew Sachs: "Jonathan Ross and Brand have ripped my family apart"'*; the article revealing Sachs' contempt for the stars behind *that* vile phone prank, his fury at their cynical 'apologies' – and how it's destroyed his relationship with his granddaughter. A suitably morbid looking photo of the actor appeared alongside.

And yet everyone, including Sachs, seemed to have been suffering a case of amnesia, as only the previous week in the same paper another headline had jubilantly exclaimed *'Andrew Sachs thanks Jonathan Ross and Russell Brand for boosting his career'*. Underneath was an equally appropriate photograph of a smiling Sachs and a story that expanded on the headline. 'I came out of it very well. My profile's up. Great! They did me good. Thank you very much,' Sachs was quoted as saying by the paper.

Therefore never underestimate the media's ability to manipulate, distort, or make up facts to get an angle, a headline or a news story, do not believe everything you read, and have no qualms about using the media to your own advantage.

Always remember...

1. Any newsworthy story usually depends on there being an element that raises it out of the commonplace.

2. A product's news value can be enhanced by creating an event around it.

3. Always try to associate your product or event with the famous or historical.

4. Never underestimate the media's ability to distort or fabrication the facts to suit a story.

STEP FIVE
CREATE A BUZZ

So now you have your product identified and have found the angle, the next thing is to tell the world about it.

This is nearly always achieved through the media and probably the most widely used single tool for providing information to them is the press release. It is cheap to produce and is relatively easy to write if you know a few basic rules. This chapter will concentrate mainly on these rules.

The ultimate aim of any press release is to be reproduced verbatim (this usually happens more in the local press) but the main objective is to get it noticed in the first place. With most national newspapers receiving hundreds of press releases a day, yours has to stand out and immediately get the interest of the person reading it. If not, it will end up on the spike – that dreaded implement on which unwanted copy is unceremoniously impaled.

The three essential elements of a good press release are a catchy headline, an equally catchy introduction and the main body of text containing your story.

The headline although at the top of the story, should paradoxically be written last. By doing this it reflects the story you have just written, rather than having to perhaps bend the story to fit the headline.

As the headline is most probably the first thing that an editor or journalist will read, this is another reason to make sure it sums up the story. This can be done by using key words from the first sentence of the introduction (which of course you would have already written by the time you tackle the headline). Two other points worth mentioning is no more than ten words maximum and always try to put a verb in it.

The next part is the opening paragraph – the introduction - and this should be two or three short sentences summing up the whole story through the five W's – who, what, where, when and why. Don't put in background information, describe the creative process or provide any anecdotes in this first paragraph.

"The biggest single fault with press releases," one seasoned journalist has bemoaned, "is that the first paragraph kills the story."

It takes practise, but writing an opening paragraph that summarises the story is relatively easy once you have the main body of text.

The five Ws mentioned above are then expanded in the rest of the press release.

The Jane Austen Centre

PRESS RELEASE

"Regency Wedding" and world record attempt at Jane Austen Festival

A Guinness World Record attempt and a real-life "Regency Wedding" are just two of the highlights on the opening Saturday of this year's Jane Austen Festival, which begins this weekend in Bath.

One of the most popular events of the festival is the Grand Regency Promenade - a spectacular costumed perambulation through the streets of Bath – and this year the several hundred Jane Austen fans it attracts from around the world will attempt to break the world record for the largest gathering of people dressed in Regency costume.

The Promenade begins at 11am on Saturday (19th) from the Roman Baths in the centre of the city and then makes its way through the Georgian streets, passing many of Bath's most famous landmarks including The Circus and Royal Crescent, before finishing in Queen Square.

This year the route also includes The Assembly Rooms, where the world record attempt will take place. After registering, all participants will remain together for ten minutes in order to successfully achieve the record.

A town crier, naval personnel and musicians will also be in attendance during the Promenade, along with re-enactment groups and societies that include members of the 32nd Cornwall Regiment and a group of hobby horse-riding enthusiasts called "The Dandy Chargers".

Also participating in the record attempt will be Kelly Walpole and Ian Charlesworth from Bury St. Edmunds, Suffolk, although the highlight of their day will come that afternoon at 4pm, when after months of preparation they will be tying the knot at their dream "Regency Wedding" at Bath's Guildhall.

The couple has invited costumed festival-goers to help celebrate their big day.

After vows have been exchanged, wedding photographs will be taken outside the Royal Crescent accompanied by a volley of shots fired by the Cornwall Regiment.

Jackie Herring, Festival Director: "With both the world record attempt and Regency wedding happening on the same day, this promises to be the best opening weekend to a Jane Austen Festival in its nine year history."

Ian Charlesworth, Groom: "We wanted to do something unusual and special for our big day, so what better than to get married during the Jane Austen Festival and be surrounded by hundreds of people dressed in Regency Costume."

Images of Jane Austen Festival is available at http://images.janeausten.co.uk/

For more information contact:
David Lassman (Press & PR Manager) 07804 246931 or press@janeausten.co.uk
Jane Austen Centre website www.janeausten.co.uk/festival

-ENDS-

NOTES TO EDITORS:

1. The Jane Austen Festival runs between 18th - 27th September with a programme of 44 events which includes walking tours, dances lesson, talks, workshop and performances.

2. The Jane Austen Festival is a popular event that attracts Jane Austen fans from all four corners of the globe. Tickets and details for all events can be found at www.janeausten.co.uk/festival.

3. Guidelines for 'Largest Gathering of People Dressed in Regency Costumes'.

All participants must be fully dressed in Regency costume outfit: Males in knee-high boots, tail or long great coats, tall neckties, floppy shirts and tight breeches; Females in full-length dresses with a high waistline, low cut necks and bonnet.

All participants must carry and wear the necessary accessories to complete the costume, e.g. hat or bonnet, reticule, gloves, Spencer jacket, pelisse or shawl. Additionally such items as a parasol, fan, cane or walking stick are not essential but can form part of the outfit.

All participants must be in position simultaneously and remain so for a minimum of 10 minutes - two experienced timekeepers will time the attempt with stopwatches accurate to 0.01 seconds.

4. All participants must wear the costume for the entirety of the attempt.

Always send an image attached with a press release as well, or at the very least a web link where it can be downloaded. As any picture is worth a thousand words this might ultimately be the difference between your story being used or not.

Local and regional media are the best places to gain publicity when starting out, especially the newspapers, as they are more likely to print a press release, well written, almost verbatim. So look at stories in your local newspaper (these should be around 200-300 words) and write one or two out as press releases to get the feel of what you should be aiming for. Try to identify the angle of the story - what has raised it out of the everyday?

With this possibility of being reprinted verbatim, it really is a golden opportunity to build a name through a series of superlatively quotes.

For example, let's say an author has organised a series of dates in order to launch a self-published book. There is a local newspaper in each of the towns he is visiting. In the first of these towns where the author is appearing, the local newspaper is called *The Smalltown Chronicle*. They are sent a short but well-written press release with all the information required and a newsworthy angle. There is also a quote somewhere in the release which reads something along the lines "A. N. Author is quickly acquiring a reputation as one of the most brilliant writers of his generation."

And who has said this - it could be his mum for all it matters. What does matter is that the local newspaper prints it. If they do, which we have seen is a distinct possibility, the author can now slightly amend the press release when sending it to *The Anywhere Gazette*, the newspaper in the next town he is visiting. This glowing accolade can now be written as a direct quote from the previous paper and could read: 'A. N. Author recently performed in Smalltown, where the local newspaper described him as 'one of the most brilliant writers of his generation.'

In this second press release, along with this quote, could be another one from his mum, perhaps along the lines of "A. N. Author possesses a dazzling writing technique rarely seen". And so on throughout the tour until at the end of it, A. N. Author has now assembled an array of perfectly genuine quotes, with the cuttings to prove it, which can be used on future publicity material.

Remember when writing your statements, modesty is the enemy of talent. Although do not claim anything that can be disproved. Bill Schneider claimed on his website and publicity material that his most recent (self-published) novel, *Crossed Paths*, had been selected for Oprah's Book Club. He also claimed that Oprah had interviewed him on her show. To prove this, he posted a full, five-page transcript of the interview. None of it, however, was true. And although he gained some publicity, along with a mention in this book, it is possible that no publisher will now take him seriously as a writer.

Another advantage of getting stories into local and regional papers is that the national papers are always scanning them for potential stories. This is exactly what happened with my Jane Austen 'experiment' story in 2007. Although a press release had been sent to all the daily newspapers and other media contacts, it was only after the story appeared in the regional Western Daily Press that it was picked up by the national media. And from there it went worldwide.

Never underestimate the power of the local and regional press.

Always remember . . .

1. The press release is the most widely used tool for providing information to the media.

2. The ultimate aim of any press release is to be reprinted verbatim.

3. Headlines on press releases should be written last, be no more than ten words, and sum up the story.

4. Opening paragraphs of press releases should include the five Ws – who, what, where, when and why.

5. Always send an image with a press release or a downloadable link.

6. Do not underestimate the importance of local and regional media.

7. Modesty is the enemy of talent but do not make any disprovable claims.

STEP SIX

BECOME NUMBER ONE

A more complete title to this chapter could have been 'Become number one in your field or create a field to become number one in'. This next step is all about what you can do to raise your profile through initiative, creative thinking and utilising opportunities as they arise.

It is said that the pen is mightier than the sword and words such as company director, international, president, leading expert, all carry with them inbuilt perceptions and connotations of power and success. It seems to be human nature that we cannot fail to be impressed if we learn someone has an important or glamorous title, even if this international film producer has yet to see any projects into production, a Hollywood screenwriter has yet to sell a film script and the managing director of a company only has one employee.

You can therefore build a profile which connects into this established way of perception and achieve a level of identity that will see others come to you or, at the very least, gain access to people and places ordinarily out of bounds. One way of doing this is to become well known for a certain role, which is probably best achieved through something related to your work.

This is one of the reasons I accepted the position of Jane Austen festival director when it was offered to me. I did think hard about accepting, as I already had a full-time job, I was studying for a qualification, I had just started a new relationship and I was working on promoting my own work, but I felt the credibility associated with the title was too good an opportunity to miss. I thought that to be the director of such an established and internationally known festival would look good on any future curriculum vitae and it was also an association with someone already very famous – Jane Austen.

It was very hard work, as I thought it would be even before I accepted the post, but as the old saying goes "the harder you work the luckier you become". And, as 'luck' would have it, a production company wanted to make a documentary about the festival that year and as festival director I ended up as one of the main interviewees.

You always have to be looking out for opportunities to become involved within your chosen field. A woman in the UK poetry scene became a local representative for the Poetry Society, after she looked through their directory, realised the nearest representative was more than 100 miles away, and put herself forward for the role.

Through these titles, you can start to be seen as an expert in a subject, which again allows your profile and image to be built on through potential media coverage. How often have you seen a story in which an expert is quoted or their opinion sought? An 'expert' gives any story credibility and therefore in turn gives credibility in the eyes of the audience to the newspaper or news programme telling it.

Of course, there is nothing to stop you creating opportunities yourself. A film director friend of mine (and yes, he has directed several films) wanted some credible endorsements for one of his projects and so he sent off promotional packs to 150 high-profile people in the industry. He only received about ten replies, but this included John Landis (*American Werewolf in London*, *The Blues Brothers*), Simon Pegg (*Hot Fuzz*) and Nicholas Roeg (*Don't Look Now*).

Along the same lines, if you are not able to have a title handed to you, then create one for yourself. I have started many organisations and have bestowed on myself an array of titles, including President of the International Eddie Cochran Appreciation Society, Editor-in-Chief of several entertainment magazines and currently director of the Bath Screen Network.

However, I am not advocating that anything you create should be a façade, like streets on a film set. For each of the organisations I have set up I produced magazines or newsletters and ran them as proper entities.

The International Eddie Cochran Appreciation Society I established, for example, published three magazines a year, based on a membership fee. At the height of its popularity 300 copies of each issue were being sent to subscribers all around the world.

This was, as I mentioned in the introduction, my first real foray into the world of publicity and media coverage, so I hope you will indulge me if I dwell on it for a while, both for practical reasons and slightly nostalgic ones.

Through an interest in early rock music in my late teens, I had joined several related societies and fan clubs for performers such as Elvis Presley, Buddy Holly and Gene Vincent.

Attempts to join Eddie Cochran ones, however, usually ended with my enquiry coming back unopened with the words 'no longer at this address' written across the envelope. It was after the third such response I thought about starting my own society. Eddie Cochran had achieved stardom young and in 1960, at the age of 21, had arrived for an English tour on the back of numerous hits, such as 'Summertime Blues', 'C'mon Everybody' and 'Twenty Flight Rock'.

After a performance in Bristol on April 16, 1960, Eddie Cochran was being driven by taxi back to London when a tyre blew out and the vehicle crashed into a lamppost near Chippenham. He was taken to a hospital in Bath, where he died the following day without regaining consciousness.

As my home town is Bath, there was already a connection with the rock star and as well as collecting the music, I also collected articles, magazines and other memorabilia connected to that period of rock history. It took me a little while to plan exactly how I was going to go about it and also to find the self-belief that I could carry it off, but finally I was ready and got to work with promoting the society.

This was the only time I have ever personally paid for advertising, taking out a small classified advert in Record Collector magazine. It cost less than a pound but the results were staggering. Most of the other people running associated fan clubs and societies read the Record Collector magazine and, as I was later to find out, formed a close-knit community. In those pre-reciprocal web-link days, they offered their support by promoting my new society in their magazines.

The society went from strength to strength and after writing the majority of articles for the early issues myself, members began to send in information, news and articles. As membership grew, so did the profile of the society and myself.

I established contacts with record labels, a Hollywood film studio, the media and several famous people; the latter mainly through the society's 'Honorary Member' list. I compiled this through keeping my ears and eyes open to anyone famous or well known who expressed an interest in Eddie's music. I then sent them honorary membership and free copies of the magazines. One high level example was politician Neil Kinnock, at the time leader of the Labour Party.

As I have also said earlier in the book, The Art of Self-Publicity is about raising your profile through association, aligning yourself with famous and well-known people until you become well-known yourself and people want to align themselves with you.

Although the society maintained a relatively high profile throughout its existence, there were two 'hotspots' which gave me very useful insights into gaining publicity and the media world.

April 1985 was the twenty-fifth anniversary of Eddie Cochran's death and thinking this might be a good newsworthy story, I tentatively approached the local media. To my perhaps somewhat naive astonishment, they grabbed it with both hands and I found myself both in print and being interviewed on radio and television. It was my first real taste of media attention and I am not afraid to say I loved every minute of it.

Major record label EMI, who owned the copyright on most of Eddie's biggest hits, decided to release a compilation album to commemorate the anniversary and put the society's address on the album sleeve (interestingly enough they fortuitously spelt one line of the address wrong, putting a 'u' instead of an 'e', which allowed me to keep track of the number of enquiries that had been generated through the album).

The other 'media highlight' came in 1988, when the jeans company Levi unveiled its 'Eddie Cochran' commercial. The advert recreated a scene from his life and used one of his greatest hits for the soundtrack. The resultant publicity saw the society's profile rise (through association) and a reporter from one of the national daily newspapers got in touch. He wanted to know whether the commercial had increased membership. What was interesting, and I became aware of this as we talked, was that he was trying to lead me into answers that would fit in with the story he wanted to write, or indeed, had already written. It was a good lesson.

At the end of the day running the society was hard work but worth it, as I learnt about the basics surrounding the mechanics of publicity and how to achieve it and I became associated with some famous people and companies.

But initiating a magazine or newsletter isn't just about creating association or raising your profile, it can be a key to allow contact with people in your own line of work that you may not ordinarily have access to.

For example, Bath Beat allowed me access to a production company through which I ended up in a rock film with the likes of Bob Dylan, Ronnie Wood, Ian Dury and many other luminaries of the music industry (and kick-started a sporadic but rewarding acting career).

It also allows you to interview people who might be able to help you or offer advice within your chosen area. When I was studying for a scriptwriting degree, I started a student newsletter called *NEWriter*. The publication raised my profile within the university and allowed me to spend more time with visiting lecturers and guests that had agreed to be interviewed for the publication. This is also a chance to get onto organisation's mailing list to find out news before the majority of the public. In the days of the internet it has become even easier, as it takes very little time to produce an e-newsletter but the rewards can be immense.

EXERCISE

1. List at least one organisation or group related your creative field within your local or regional area that you could join

2. List two things you could do to enhance your profile within your local area

3. List a possible organisation or group related to your creative field that you could start

---

As you may well have realised, it is all about making that first contact and gaining access. It is said there is no front door in publishing, or indeed any creative industry, so you must create the window or back door through which you can get inside. And once there is personal contact with someone, be it through an interview request or other 'legitimate' reason, it becomes much easier to gain access.

What hopefully all this should be saying is that whatever area you are interested in pursuing you should acquire as big a title as quickly as possible. If you are the president, company director, international secretary or editor-in-chief of some organisation or other, you are more likely to establish access with a valuable contact than if you are just another random 'nobody'.

Put even blunter, if you have an important enough sounding title you will be perceived as being in a position of power and therefore in a more likely position to also help the person you are contacting. Remember the reporter who needs an expert quote, for example. You provide a quote and this raises your profile through the story. The reporter, through using it, gives the article credibility and by association his own credibility and that of his paper increases also.

You may be surprisingly amazed how easy it is to make contact through interviewing industry people but it is really simple psychology – most people like to talk about themselves and if you are giving them an opportunity to do so, they will often agree to it.

As you build your profile, so the level of possible contacts widens. Back in the mid-1990s, when I was involved in establishing a regional version of the Big Issue, I saw an article about a local musician who was trying to put together a compilation tape of local bands – he rightly assumed strength in numbers might give it a bigger impact in terms of media coverage and the fact he was compiling it also would lend him some kudos in the eyes of the music business.

To cut a long story short we met and it was decided the compilation would be released to raise money for The Big Issue. As the brand was already well-known in London and had caused quite a stir, in a positive way, this allowed us access to 'named' local bands as well.

The end result was that the eventual release combined groups such as The Stranglers, Julian Cope and Strangelove – all local to the south-west region – and a number of unsigned groups. The musician with the original idea naturally included his own group and they recorded a specially written song for the album.

This was the angle that got the media interested, as the song was recorded at a major studio in the area with some of the more musical Big Issue sellers providing backing vocals. The story was reported by the media throughout the region.

So therefore always be looking for opportunities through which you can raise your profile and make valuable contacts.

Always remember...

1. Certain titles carry with them inbuilt perceptions and connotations of power and success.

2. The harder you work the luckier you seem to become.

3. Being seen as an expert on something immediately raises your profile.

4. Any titles you can bestow on yourself or organisations you create should have a solid foundation to them.

5. Magazines and newsletters allow the chance to contact certain people otherwise inaccessible.

6. Always be looking for opportunities within your chosen field to raise your profile.

STEP SEVEN

SUSTAINING YOUR PROFILE

I believe with the diversification and proliferation of media outlets and numerous sources of communication, it has never been easier to create a substantial profile for oneself in a short time – the hard part is sustaining it.

Remember, self-publicity isn't just the column inches in the newspapers it is also the poster in the newsagent's window; it is about getting your name visible in every location you can. As mentioned earlier in the book, no one will be a greater cheerleader than yourself and no one but you will, or should, work harder to achieve your success.

Whatever else Jeffrey Archer may be, he has proved himself to be one of the great self-publicists. His exploits are numerous and legendary, but one story has stuck with me as proof of how hard he works to sustain his profile. During the early days of his career as an author, so the story goes, he made a point of talking to every book stand owner at the train stations he frequented and was rewarded, through this small and perhaps innocuous piece of PR, by seeing his books at the front of the stand the following time he visited.

You must therefore become your biggest fan and tell as many people as possible about yourself and your work. The place through which to reach the widest audience is, of course, the internet.

For all the events you attend, the quotes you achieve and countless reams of column inches you generate, it is perhaps a universal truth these days that if you haven't got a web presence you do not really exist.

There is no real excuse for not having a web presence and every artist if they are serious about their work, needs one. The first thing I always do when I make a new contact is to look them up on a search engine to find out more about them (and I know many people who attend my workshops do likewise). This society has been called the 'Google' generation after all. So let the world know you exist.

The search engine is perhaps the main component to having a web presence and it cannot be over-emphasised how important this tool is for raising your profile. If someone taps in your name, or your company, into a search engine, you have to make sure that it is your name and what you do that appears as the first entry in the results (and preferably a couple more times also in the first ten entries. This usually equates to the first page of results that you see on your computer screen and beyond which the majority of users do not tend to go).

Obviously if you share a name with Elvis Presley, Marilyn Monroe or William Shakespeare then you have to make sure you become known through some other way. This could be using a company name, an alter ego or such like. Whatever you choose to use, it has to get you in the first page of results and ultimately the top spot.

I regularly check search engines to see how often in the first few pages of results my name or associated events appear but make a point of viewing the initial two pages from a google search the night before a workshop.

I have a relatively unusual name, although certainly not unique, but I was pleased checking one evening before a particular workshop to see I held 13 out of the first 20 results. What was really satisfying was these included the entire first page of results and had been achieved through various sources. A number of results related to the Jane Austen 'experiment' story, but also my workshops, my website, a Wikipedia article on me, the festival documentary and a talk I was due to give at a literary event.

Important as search engines are to sustaining your profile, so is having a website. A website is the fundamental tool to having a web presence. If you don't have one, you risk the possibility of not being taken seriously. The website doesn't have to be complicated - a home page with an email address attached may suffice - but to have a dedicated site where people can visit and find out about you is essential. It also provides a place where you can display examples of your work.

If the whole thought of having a website is daunting, do not worry. It can be relatively simple, although you will need to spend some time to plan what kind of site it is you want and to decide what domain name you want. A domain name comes between the www and .co.uk or .com to create a unique website address - mine is www.davidlassman.com.

Much of this planning time will be used looking at websites of other artists to see what you like or dislike about them (the design that is, not the actual artists). Can you read the text easily, do the pages feel too 'busy' and are there too many images and not enough information. All these things play a factor and it is best to make notes as you go through.

EXERCISE

1. Make a list of three relevant websites you have visited and one thing about each that you liked and one thing that you disliked.

2. Make a list of where you have a web presence (e.g. facebook, own website etc) and then make a list of three other outlets where you could have one.

3. Tap your name into a search engine and look at the first page of results. How many of them are yours? How many people with the same name as you are there? What do they do and how have they achieved their entries?

4. List three places you could meet other relevant people in your local area.

Once you know the kind of website you want, you have to decide whether to get someone else to design and run it, or do it all yourself. I have a presence on various websites and these are mainly taken care of by other people but my official website I do run myself. Personally, I find it quicker and easier to add, delete or amend information rather than perhaps having to wait for someone else to implement changes.

If you decide to go down the do-it-yourself route, basic web-design can be easily grasped. There are a couple of rules to remember before you begin though. Do not use too many different typefaces as this can be difficult on the eye - the key to a good website is to make the experience for visitors to your site a pleasurable one. Try not to superimpose text onto an image or include large images that may take a long time to download onto the screen and remember that black or dark-coloured text on a white background is always the easiest to read.

Once the website is online, you have to maintain it. I apportion a certain amount of my time to updating the site, as I want people to visit regularly and the only way to do this is by providing them with new information. A monthly diary is one way that I encourage people to return. It cannot be overstated that a website is really your shop front to the world, so make the most of it.

Social networks are also an essential tool for raising your profile and spreading information about yourself. However, you have to be strict in recognising this as part of an ongoing publicity campaign, so maintaining a professional attitude, and not get caught up in the 'social' side.

Blogs, journals, diaries and newsletters are also effective ways to create interest in you and attract possible buyers for your work. I send out a monthly e-newsletter with all work-related activities and this goes out to a mailing list I have compiled from the various workshops, talks and other events I have been involved in. When I lived on a Greek Island I published a regular journal on my day to day life there and this was read by people from around the world. Whatever you write or send out though, don't forget to always include your website address somewhere in the text, even if it's just within your email signature.

There are many, many outlets for raising your profile on the internet, far too many to list in this book, but an hour or two surfing with a professional objective will no doubt yield a number of possibilities each time.

However, there is still nothing better than face to face contact so as well as the internet, always be networking in the 'real' world and try not to miss any relevant opportunities to meet people. This connects with an earlier chapter where you found out about groups and organisations in your area. And even though some of these activities you may become involved in seem almost grass roots, never forget in terms of your profile, it's from small acorns that large trees grow.

Always remember . . .

1. It has never been easier to create a substantial profile.

2. You must become your biggest fan.

3. There is no excuse for not having a web presence.

4. The search engine is the key to your profile on the web.

5. A website is essential for a web presence and to be taken seriously.

6. Sustaining a profile will be hard work but rewarding.

7. Social networks, on and off the web, should be fully utilised in sustaining your profile.

...AND FINALLY

The level of self-publicity you achieve each time will no doubt vary and any opportunities to gain media coverage will probably be seen in terms of importance. However, I have always found it is important to treat every opportunity or resultant exposure the same.

With this mind, never refuse an interview (or opportunity to talk about your work) if you can help it. Be flexible. And always make sure when planning any publicity campaign that you are available for interviews.

Try to have a long term plan regarding your profile building, as without one it will be like a rudder-less boat on the ocean, bobbing around with no real destination.

As much as an artist needs their ego, do not start believing your own publicity. Keep a detached and observational eye on it. If you have to, create a persona or an alter ego that can be hung up on the coat rack when you go home each night.

Author Celia Brayfield has these three sobering points - fame should not be a licence to behave boorishly, be nice to your peers, and try not to act like a prat!

And finally, finally, take the bad with the good and always remember whatever you do may be around for a long time, as newspapers and other media outlets have press files where they can use cuttings of previous stories as background information for later ones.

When I was living on a small Greek island in 2005, a reporter from the newspaper back in my home town of Bath got in touch by email. It was regarding a story they were writing about the forty-fifth anniversary of Eddie Cochran's death and having no doubt pulled out old cuttings had found my name. And even though I had stopped running his appreciation society almost fifteen years before, they still wanted to interview me and get some quotes for the local connection. (This shows the power of the internet as discussed in the previous chapter, as the reporter tracked me down through an unrelated website I was involved with at the time after putting my name in a search engine).

It is the same for photographs - you never know when one might return to haunt you. For me, there is a particular image that resurfaces every so often in various publications. It was taken one lunch-time when I was director of the Jane Austen festival and even though people have tried to convince me it doesn't look that bad, I cringe a little every time I see it.

You have been warned.

Writers' Workshop Guides are designed for all creative people. Practical, easy-to-follow and easy on the pocket, they are written by experts, and offer the essentials in a 'no-nonsense' format; everything you need to get started in a nutshell.

For a list of forthcoming titles contact Awen.

Send a SAE to: Awen Publications, 7 Dunsford Place, Bath BA2 6HF. For paper free version: email publisher@awenpublications.co.uk or check the website: www.awenpublications.co.uk